Fly

Written and illustrated by

Amanda Wiltshire

JABIRU
PUBLISHING

PO Box 188N, Cairns North, QLD 4870, Australia
www.jabirupublishing.com.au

ISBN: 9780648250104

Cover designed by Stephen Shaw, Shawcreate, www.shawcreate.co.uk
Cover photograph by Amanda Wiltshire
Text editing and design by Wordfix, www.word-fix.com.au
Century 11
Printed in Australia by Kaligraphic Print,
www.kaligraphicprint.com.au

Copies may be purchased from www.helenwiltshiregallery.com.au
and www.jabirupublishing.com.au

YES
I have witnessed
emotional and financial abuse
heartbreak
difficulty leaving a toxic relationship
separated/broken family
divorce
death
cancer
financial hardship
unfulfilling work

I am grateful I have compassion
for others experiencing these life events.
This book is intended to help others so that they may
understand their own circumstances and move quickly
out of a negative situation into love, joy and peace.
I want to lift you up so you can
FLY!

Change

Even prisoners become nervous about the idea of being released,
as moving out of a comfort zone can be daunting. Be willing to
accept change, and release yourself from the place where your mind
often tries to keep you in a state of fear or negativity.
Leaving home, particularly for young adults, can often be delayed
by the comfort that is provided in most modern-day homes.
It is also often very difficult for parents to "let their children go".
The bond created over time becomes a vacant space in the physical
sense, which can be difficult to adjust to. As a parent, recognise
that love always needs a place to go, and channel that energy into
your own passions. Your children will thank you
for giving them the opportunity to "grow up".
The same applies to unhappy relationships.
Imagine your dream life and set sail. Having times of quiet
and silence will help you imagine what to do
that keeps you happy and enjoying life.
Don't let the comforts of the nest get in the way of starting life,
or setting off on a new journey or experience.

Finding Your Passion

Always return to your own quiet time to ask yourself questions;
it is a place to reset your compass.

Meditation is often found within sport, in art,
and in contemplation.

You have the ability at any one time to choose your thoughts,
to focus on a chosen thought. Meditation, art, sport or your most
peaceful zone provides a heavenly break for the brain and the
body. This is when people can take their talents to the next
level, as they are allowing a flow that comes naturally
without thought.

It is in these moments that our bodies are at their happiest.
It is the natural state of the body to be in that zone.

Love

Follow your heart

Love one hundred percent.

You may get hurt by love; you will likely glow with love;
you may be heartbroken by love. These are natural processes
that allow you to understand the tenderness of the heart,
for you to be tender and understanding of life.

In order to achieve true personal growth, you need to fully open
your heart and love like you have never been hurt.
Allow this to take place.

Love is not words alone but is backed by action.

Love is caring on a deep level;
true love is the reciprocation of love.

Marriage and Partnerships

Once you find love, try not to make an unhealthy bond. Allow, encourage and foster individuality, while sharing joys and sorrows together. Enjoy time alone. There is no ownership of another person or the direction of love. Love has its own course. Be grateful for love.

Be able to let love go if it has no chance of return. It would be honourable to have and give the freedom to leave a relationship if either party is not happy. True love would not want the other to be unhappy. Vows should not override that freedom; vows may be best written in terms of "for as long as we both are happy".

Remember that all life ends; and with it, love ends in the physical sense. Allow a relationship to end sooner if that is necessary, should reciprocated love be gone.

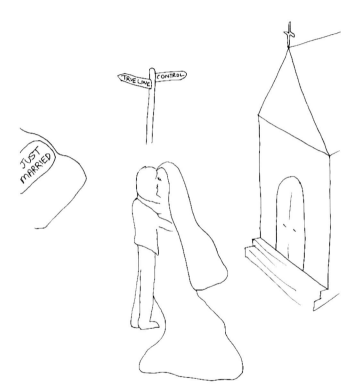

Children

Children do not belong to you as a parent.
Give them your love and shelter; let them think on their own;
accept their differences from you.
Remember: they are not you.
Remember that they notice every word you say and every move you
make. They feel the mood in the room. Children are deeply affected
by their surroundings. Be aware as an adult of the presence of
children. Give praise whenever possible so that their self-esteem is
able to grow in a positive way. If the only talk is negative, it will
suffocate their will to enjoy the breath of life that they are so very
entitled to. Negativity seems to compound over time and rears
itself often many years later; the person is left to wonder why they
are not happy, having covered over but not dealt with the hurt
attached to negativity at a young age.
Each child who is born is innocent and deserves love that is true
love, acted, spoken love, love capable of being received as love.
So often, children are given material possessions
but not given love, when all they want is love.

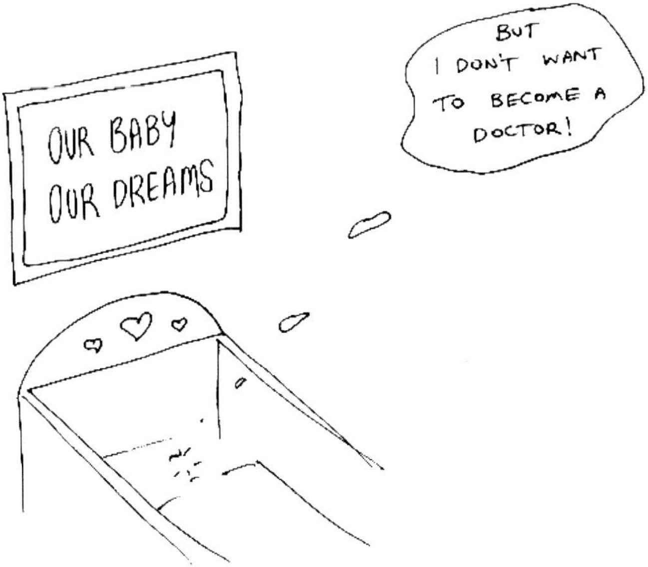
OUR BABY
OUR DREAMS
BUT I DON'T WANT TO BECOME A DOCTOR!

Giving

Giving of possessions is easy.
Giving yourself is when you truly give; give time, care, love.

Gifts given for recognition take away from giving.
Sharing spreads the joy and beauty of life; joy is a reward.
Possessing things can be an unquenchable thirst, never enough.
Be grateful for what you have or you will always be dissatisfied.
Just as houses are places of shelter, not true comfort,
no love will come from an empty building.
Where possible, exchange or swap goods and services.
Include others and create satisfaction of the soul.

Money is a commodity that goes up and down; it is not who you
are. Don't get too caught up in the belief that money is success,
for when the tables turn (and they inevitably will)
you will reconsider the importance of money.

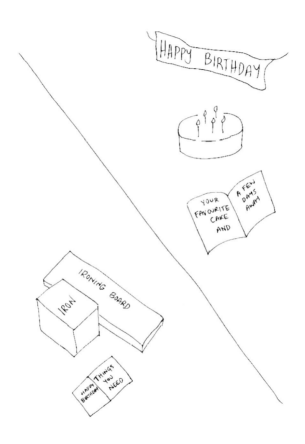

Health

If you choose to eat meat and drink milk (by the way, that milk
is meant for the animal's newborn), be aware of what has
occurred for that food to be provided. Even with fresh foods,
wine, water, be aware that the earth has provided such goods
and be grateful to take part in enjoying these.
Use food to fuel your body with healthy choices, as the food you
eat impacts your whole body, including your mind. Be very
aware of your diet if you are unwell, either physically or
mentally. Make changes to improve your body; take
responsibility for your own health. Increase fresh fruits and
vegetables as these foods are a source of nutrition and energy
for the body. Your health is also very much a reflection of your
emotional state. If you are unwell or sick, ask yourself why.
Be truly honest with yourself.
Don't pretend everything is all right when it's not.
Take steps to change, to improve your health
by improving your happiness.
Your body will react in a negative way if you are not happy.

There are direct links between health,
and emotional health and happiness.
If you are abusing your body by over-consumption of food,
alcohol or drugs, ask yourself why would you want to damage
your own body; investigate what is behind the choice
you make for yourself.

Work

Work should not be unpleasant; by working you are living and loving life. To love life through work is one of the greatest achievements.

Electing not to work will make you stagnant, and you will miss out on so much of life that can be an overwhelmingly positive and rewarding experience.

When you love your work, you are truly at your best.
Build a house or cook as if it were for your true love.
Your results are love made visible.

Think about what it is that you would happily volunteer to do – this is where your passion lies. If you can do that for work, you have discovered a joy.

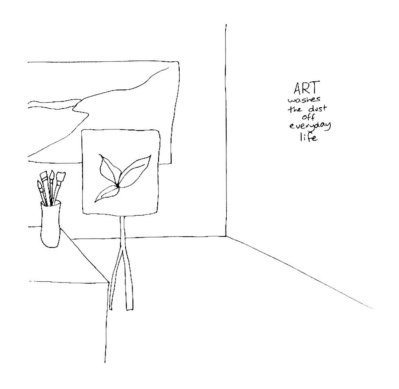

ART
washes
the dust
off
everyday
life

Happy and Sad

Having been sad allows you to know happiness, which is a joyous feeling in comparison, intrinsically linked when fully analysed. It rises and falls; one replaces the other.

Sadness is a season, just as the weather has seasons. Accept that it comes and goes. Sadness creates an understanding of the experience, which enables us to have compassion and caring for others, with true depth to our caring and understanding.
If you can't get through your sad times, seek help; start by talking about it. Very often, so many before you have gone through a similar situation, and they are so very well-equipped to help you. A strong friendship can be built on overcoming an adversity together. Often, another person has a solution to your problem, one that you were unable to come up with, even though on reflection it would seem to be a simple or obvious choice.
We are often unable to make that decision when frozen in a state of anxiety.

Your Beautiful Body

Remember that bodies are beautiful, and they relish in the
outdoors. Be proud of your body; in its natural state
it is truly beautiful.

Don't let others abuse your body. If you feel uncomfortable,
change the situation until you are comfortable.

Take ownership of the health of your body.
Allow comfortable sunlight onto your skin
and be barefoot on the earth.
Being in nature and a part of nature
is a perfectly healthy choice.
Youth by itself is beautiful.

Be confident of your beauty, including your inner beauty.

Compassion

All people are capable of making wrong choices;
understand and have compassion in all circumstances.
Avoid making judgement.
Be kind always.

In order to live peacefully you must follow your passion,
as this is when you are in a true state of happiness,
and the mind has no time to take over your thoughts.

When resting, the mind should rest;
when moving, it should be with passion.

Greatness

We all have the capability to be great, but in different ways.

Greatness takes time to develop, and no comparisons with others can be made, as for each person this maturity into greatness is so different, and the timing is so varied, that it makes us unique.

You are unique.

Friendship

Connecting with friends is refreshing.
Laugh and share, live and enjoy.

Use the gift of speech to express your innermost feelings.
Speech is one of the greatest tools of learning and loving.

Share your problems with a friend;
by doing so you will ease your own burden,
and very likely an alternative viewpoint
to your problem can reveal a solution.

Time

Yesterday, today, tomorrow.

Contemplation will stretch time like no other pastime.

Daydream often.
Enjoy such moments for they truly last the longest.

Take steps towards your dreams.

Exercise

Go to the gym or wherever you can to do exercise. Better still,
do your exercise experiencing nature, and double your benefits:
barefoot walking on the beach, swimming in the ocean,
walks in the park. Enjoy what nature has to offer.

Try to avoid stress. If racing to a gym class becomes a stress –
"I have to be there by 8.30" – change your exercise plan;
re-evaluate your planning to avoid stress.
There are plenty of options.
You can even exercise at home if you find that easier.
Whatever works for you, your body will be thankful for,
as exercise does provide rewards directly to the body.

If you want your body to go the distance – eighty, ninety years
or more – then you need to keep some flexibility and agility.
If you are expecting to maintain physical capability, then start
investing time and energy into maintaining your health.

Good and Bad

We all have those capabilities and times.

Each person is capable of both good and bad.

Be understanding of the other.

Allow others to be and do at their own pace.

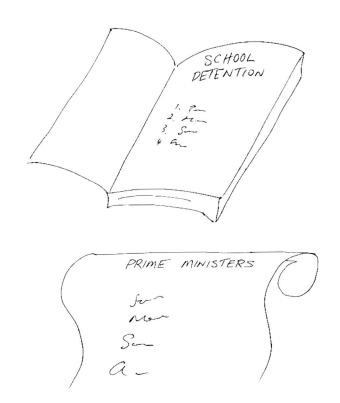

Positive Thinking

Be it a prayer, an affirmation or a simple thought,
positive thinking is the way to a positive life.
It is important to take time for positivity.

Enjoy life's pleasures, but be sure to give and receive.
Life is beautiful, and that life is in each one of us.

Worry is the alternative, and often too much negative thought
brings a negative result.

LIGHT
FOR
LOVE

LIGHT A CANDLE
AND PRAY
FOR MORE LOVE
IN THE WORLD

Religion

Whatever your religion, live it each day.
See the beauty of what you believe in, in everyday life,
so evident in all living things.
God or no God, life is extraordinary.

Agree to disagree on religious beliefs, as we are each
entitled to believe or not.
The similarity is that we are all humans
seeking our happy place.

Death

Don't fear this event of death, even though it is a mystery,
the completion and pinnacle of a life's journey, a natural event,
just as birth is a natural event.

Our bodies are a physical presence; yet our spirit is not.
Spirit is greater and unseen,
vast and everlasting.

Imagine death as a stepping stone, that you are not confined
to your body in life or in death. Imagine the spirit has a one-way
mirror into our world. They are with us but can't been seen.
Be a free spirit in life and in death.

Be open also to the spirit being born again after death
in another form – a new life, a joyous event.
Recognise the absolute joy and beauty
that surround each new life.

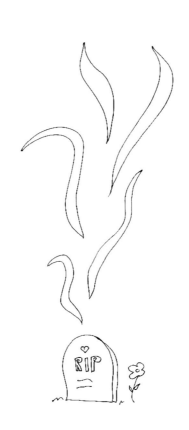

Intuition

Intuition is about instinct, recognising your body's ability to pick up on things. Be very aware of your physical reaction. If it feels wrong, then that is your instinct connecting with you. Similarly, if it feels right.

Often the gut is the centre of intuitive response.

Humans can obtain more detail by interpreting their dreams or visions, or even connecting with spirit – a very magical world to those open enough and brave enough to enter that space.

Never be quick to write off the supernatural
as impossible or untrue;
if we can think it, then it is possible,

Keep in contact with your intuition for it is your magic;
it belongs to you.